# Drawing

## Sue Nicholson

QEB Publishing, Inc.

Published in the United States by
QEB Publishing, Inc.
23062 La Cadena Drive
Laguna Hills, CA 92653

www.qeb-publishing.com

Library of Congress Control Number: 2005921169

ISBN 1-59566-083-6

Written by Sue Nicholson
Designed by Susi Martin
Editor Paul Manning

Publisher Steve Evans
Creative Director Louise Morley
Editorial Manager Jean Coppendale

Printed and bound in China

The author and publisher would like to thank Billy and Dylan Sarah Morley for making the models.

Picture credits
**Corbis** /Caroline Penn 6, /Kevin Fleming 19, /Richard Cummings 22
**Getty Images** /Steve Bly/Stone 15, /Bridgeman Art Library 17
**The Art Archive** /Musée des Arts Africains et Océaniens /Dagli Orti 13
**Travelsite** /Neil Setchfield 9, 11
**Werner Forman/British Museum** 21

## Note to teachers and parents

The projects in this book are aimed at children in grades 1–3 and are presented in order of difficulty, from easy to more challenging. Each can be used as a stand-alone activity or as part of another area of learning.

While the ideas in the book are offered as inspiration, children should always be encouraged to work from their own imagination and first-hand observations.

### Sourcing ideas

★ Encourage the children to source ideas from their own experiences as well as from magazines, books, the Internet, art galleries, or museums.

★ Urge them to talk about different types of art they have seen at home or on vacation.

★ Use the "Click for Art!" boxes as a starting point for finding useful material on the Internet.*

★ Suggest that each child keep a sketchbook of his or her ideas.

### Evaluating work

★ Encourage the children to share their work and talk about their ideas and ways of working. What do they like best/least about it? If they did it again, what would they do differently?

★ Help the children judge the originality of their work and appreciate the different qualities in others' work. This will help them value ways of working that are different from their own.

★ Encourage the children by displaying their work.

* Website information is correct at the time of going to press. However, the publishers cannot accept liability for information or links found on third-party websites.

# Contents

Words in bold, **like this**, are explained in the Glossary on page 24.

# Getting started

In this book, you'll learn how to make your drawings better. All you need are a few basic materials.

## Top tip

Always carry a **sketchbook** with you for quick on-the-spot drawing. You can turn your work into finished pictures later.

**Eraser**

**Drawing pencils**

## Drawing materials

Pencils come in different grades. Look for the numbers and letters on the side.

2H = Hard. Good for light, sharp lines and details
HB = Medium-hard. Good for sketching
2B = Soft. Good for wide, soft lines and shading

An eraser is used for erasing pencil lines.

Charcoal is good for quick, bold sketches.

Chalk comes in different colors. Use it for sketches or to color in large areas.

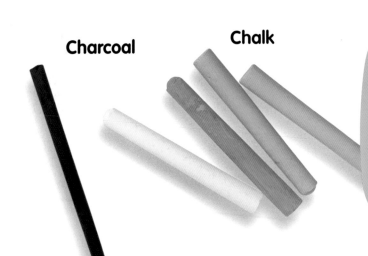

**Charcoal**

**Chalk**

## Top tip

Try using different materials and papers. A thick, soft pencil, charcoal, or chalk on rough paper gives an interesting **texture**.

## Pastels

## Colored pencils

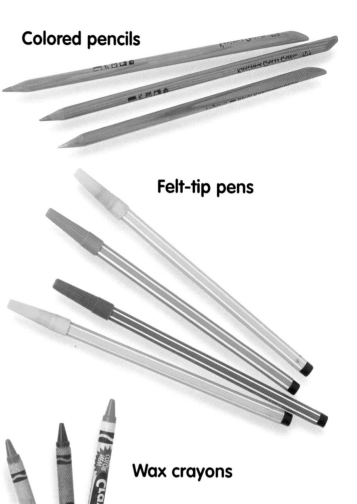

## Felt-tip pens

## Wax crayons

## Pastel paper

## Sketch paper

Pastels can be oil or chalk. Oil pastels are brighter, but both types are soft and crumbly. You can smudge pastels to make blurred lines.

Felt-tip pens are useful for adding detail and strong black lines.

Wax crayons come in lots of different colors. They are good for bold, colorful pictures.

## Paper

You can draw on many types of paper. Smooth **sketch paper** is best for pen and pencil drawings.

**Pastel paper** is good for charcoal, chalk, pastels, and crayons.

### Safety tips
Sharpen pencils with a pencil sharpener. Use safety scissors when cutting paper.

# Pencil work

Make your drawings more realistic and **three-dimensional** by adding **shading** and **highlights**.

## Top tip

For an interesting texture, try shading with the side of a pencil or the wide edge of the charcoal.

## Shading and highlights

Shading is a way of making parts of a picture look darker.

You can erase parts of your shading and make shiny, white highlights with an eraser.

## Smoky steam train

Look at this drawing of a steam train made with charcoal.

Charcoal smudged with a fingertip to make smoke

Front of train heavily shaded to look darker

Shading erased to make highlights

Short, spiky lines for grass

**Click for Art!**

To see a drawing by van Gogh, go to **www.ibiblio.org/wm/paint/auth/gogh/fields/** Scroll down and click on "Wheat Field with Sun and Cloud."

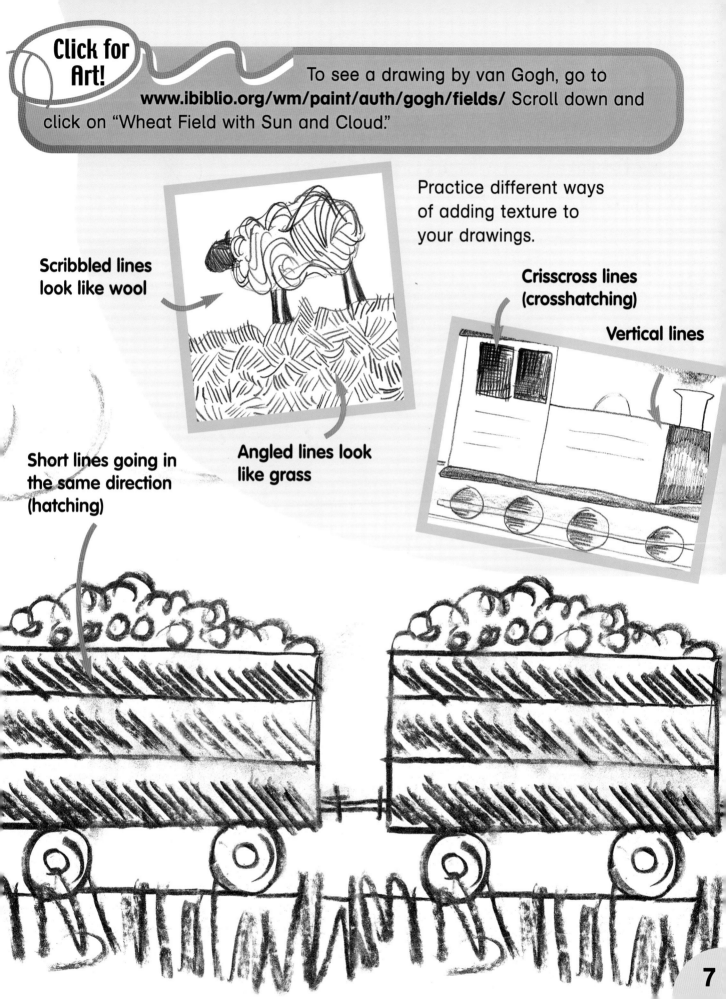

Practice different ways of adding texture to your drawings.

**Scribbled lines look like wool**

**Crisscross lines (crosshatching)**

**Vertical lines**

**Short lines going in the same direction (hatching)**

**Angled lines look like grass**

7

# Self-portrait

A self-portrait is a picture of YOU, the artist. Making a self-portrait is a good way to learn how to draw faces.

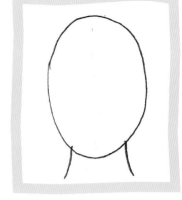

**1** Using a soft pencil, lightly draw an egg shape for the outline of your face.

## Using a mirror

Take a good look at your face in a large mirror. Try smiling, then frowning, then looking sad. Watch how your **features** change.

**Click for Art!**

To see a self-portrait by Peter Blake, go to **www.tate.org.uk/collection/** Search on "Peter Blake," "Self-portrait with Badges." To see a self-portrait by Frida Kahlo, go to **www.artchive.com/artchive/K/kahlo/kahlo_trotsky.jpg.html**

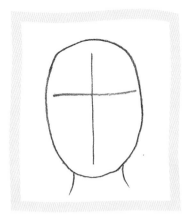

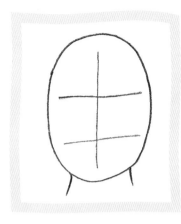

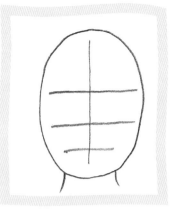

**2** Lightly draw one line down the middle of the oval. Draw a second line across the middle for the eyes.

**3** Draw another line from side to side for the tip of the nose. This should be halfway between the eye line and the chin.

**4** Draw another line between the nose line and the chin. This is where the mouth will go.

**5** Use the lines as a guide to sketch in your features. Start with the eyes. Most people's are more than one eye-width apart.

**7** Add your other features—eyelashes, eyebrows, ears, and hair. Usually the bottom of your ears will be level with the tip of your nose.

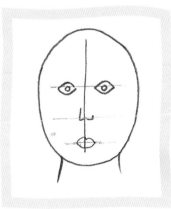

**6** Now draw your mouth and the tip of your nose.

**8** Add some shading using colored pencils, crayons, or chalk.

**Self-portrait by Drew, age 6.**

## Top tip

When drawing a face, be careful to get the eyes, mouth, and nose in the right place. Often, people draw the eyes too high up or too far apart.

# Drawing people

When you draw people, start with simple shapes such as ovals, circles, and oblongs.

**1** Draw an oval for the head at the top of your paper.

**2** Add a tube for the neck. Make it almost as wide as the head.

## Me and my grandma

Draw a picture of yourself with someone special—a brother, sister, grandparent, or best friend.

Remember to build up the bodies with circles and ovals. Make the shapes light so you can erase them later.

**Click for Art!**

To see chalk drawings by Watteau, go to **www.getty.edu/art/collections/bio/a365-1.html**

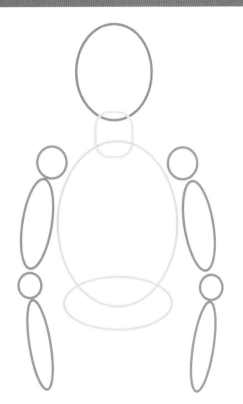

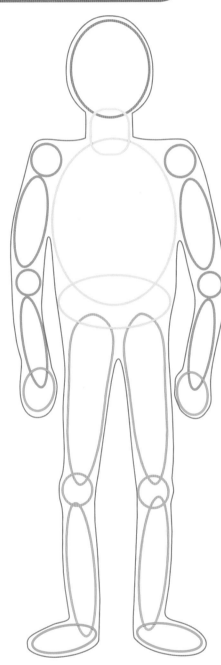

**3** Add a large oval for the top part of the body and a smaller oval for the hips.

**4** Draw circles for the shoulders, oblong shapes for the upper arms, more circles for the elbows, and oblongs for the lower parts of the arms.

**5** Add the legs in the same way. Make the ovals wider at the top. Add circles for knees, then thinner oblong shapes for the shins.

**6** Add simple hand and feet shapes, then finish off with the body's **outline**.

## Top tip

Find photos or cut pictures of people out of magazines. Practice drawing their bodies by using simple shapes.

# Drawing movement

Here's how to make a cardboard figure to help you draw people in different positions.

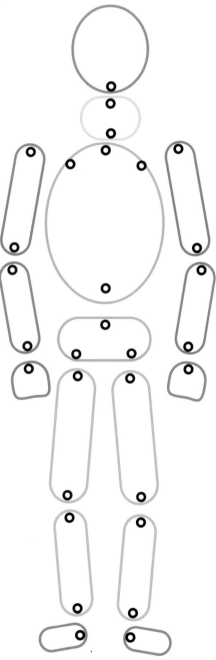

**Trace these shapes onto tracing paper, then white cardboard**

**I** Trace the shapes on the left onto tracing paper, then transfer them to cardboard.

**2** Using safety scissors, cut out the cardboard shapes. Push a small hole in each shape with the tip of a ballpoint pen and fasten the shapes together with paper fasteners.

**3** Move the parts of your cardboard body so that it looks like it is running, jumping, or kicking a ball.

**4** Use the figure to help you draw body shapes in different positions, or trace around the figure.

## You will need:
- Tracing paper
- White cardboard
- Paper fasteners

**Arrange the figure so the body looks like it is moving naturally**

# speed lines

Speed lines will help bring your moving body to life.

If you add straight speed lines, the figure will look as if it is flashing past you.

If you add curved speed lines, the figure will look as if it is twirling or twisting around.

**Click for Art!**

To see how artists have drawn moving bodies, go to **www.artlex.com** Click on "Mol–MZ" and scroll down to "movement' or 'motion."

# Furry animals

You can draw animals in the same way as people, using simple shapes such as circles, ovals, and triangles.

**Top tip**
Real animals are hard to draw because they never keep still! Collect animal pictures in a scrapbook so you can look carefully at the animals' shapes.

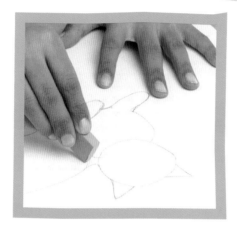

**1** Draw simple shapes such as circles and ovals first. Make sure the animal's head is smaller than its body.

**2** Draw an outline around the shapes. Erase lines you no longer need.

**3** Add details such as the ears, eyes, nose, and whiskers.

## Drawing fur

To make animals look lifelike, you need to draw the texture of their fur. Here are some different ways.

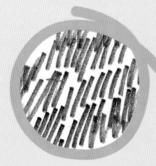

**Velvety-smooth fur drawn with a soft brown oil pastel**

**Short, spiky fur drawn with a fine felt-tip pen**

**Soft, fluffy fur drawn with oil pastel**

**Shaggy fur drawn with scribbled pencil lines**

14

**Click for Art!**

For animal drawings by Beatrix Potter,
go to **www.peterrabbit.co.uk/beatrixpotter/beatrixpotter1c_a.cfm**
For an outline drawing of a wolf, go to **www.tate.org.uk/collection/** and
search on "Henri Gaudier-Brzeska, A Wolf."

Here are some other furry animals
for you to sketch.

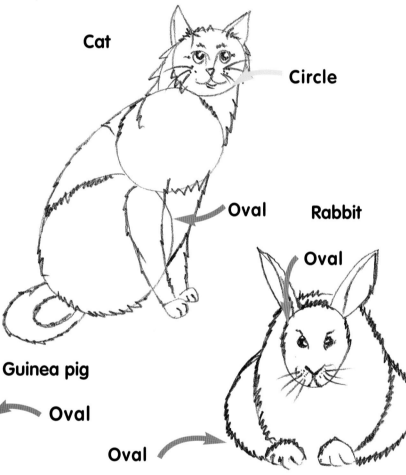

**Cat**

Circle

Oval

**Rabbit**

Oval

**4** Add color and texture
for the fur. Look at the
yellow box for ways of
drawing fur.

**Guinea pig**

Oval

Circle

Oval

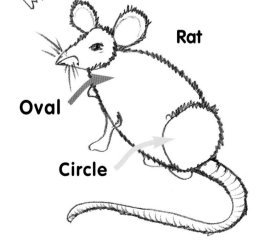

**Rat**

Oval

Circle

## Top tips

Lines and dots can be
smudged with your fingertip
to make a cat's fur look soft.

Try erasing small areas of
shading with an eraser
to make highlights.

**15**

# Fish, reptiles, and birds

You can draw fish, reptiles, and birds in the same way as cats and dogs, using simple shapes.

**Top tip**
Birds are the easiest pets to draw—all you need is a circle for the head, an oval body, and a long pointed tail.

## Bird

**1** Draw a circle and an oval.
**2** Add the wing and tail shapes.
**3** Add the eye, beak, and feet.

## Fish face

**1** Draw an oval head.
**2** Draw two bulging eyes on both sides, and a curved mouth.
**3** Add the tail and fins.

## Snake

**1** Start with a simple curved line.
**2** Draw the rest of the body.
**3** Add the snake's eye, tongue, and markings.

# scales and feathers

Scales can be drawn neatly, in rows. Notice how scales often overlap each other. You can add some shading, too.

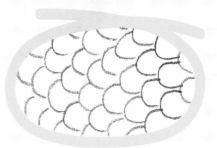

Use long, straight lines to draw large feathers on a bird's wings and tail.

## Lizard

1 Draw two ovals and a tail.
2 Add the legs.
3 Draw patterns on the lizard's body. Don't forget its tongue!

Use short, curved lines to draw short, soft feathers on a bird's head and chest.

## Turtle

1 Draw half an oval for the shell and the head.
2 Add the legs and neck.
3 Draw markings on the shell and legs.

**Click for Art!**

To see children's drawings of birds and snakes, go to **www.junglephotos.com/** Click on "Lots more!," then follow the link to "Children's artwork/St. Mary Magdalene School."

# Cities

City streets are full of exciting shapes. Follow the steps below to make your own city scene.

## You will need:

- A large sheet of sketch paper
- Wax crayons or pastels
- A soft pencil
- A ruler

## Top tip

The next time you visit a big city, look carefully at the buildings. What do you notice about the shapes of doors, windows, and roofs?

**1** Lightly sketch the outline of different buildings across the bottom of the paper.

**2** Draw taller buildings behind. Use a ruler to keep your lines straight.

# City at night

This picture of a city at night has been drawn with bright red, yellow, white, and blue crayons on black paper.

**Curved sides of buildings make the picture look more exciting**

**Tiny colored dashes for lit-up windows**

**3** Sketch in building details, such as doors and windows. Make details smaller in the **background**, so some buildings look farther away.

**4** Go over the outlines of your buildings in wax crayons or pastels. Use a different color for each building.

**5** Color in the rest of your picture using strong, bright colors. Paint a blue sky behind your city, or cut out a row of buildings and glue it to a sheet of colored paper.

**Click for Art!**

To see Robert Delaunay's "The Red Tower," go to **www.artchive.com/artchive/D/delaunay/red_tower.jpg.html**

# Countryside

In the country, shapes are rounded and softer than in the city. Follow the steps to draw a scene with different tree shapes and rounded hills.

**1** Lightly sketch the shape of the trees (look at the green box for help)

## You will need:
- A large sheet of sketch paper
- Colored chalks, pastels, or crayons

**2** Draw the rounded hills. Make them smaller as they get farther away.

**3** Draw the shapes of smaller trees in the distance.

**4** Color in the drawing with chalks, pastels, or crayons.

# Drawing trees

**1** Lightly sketch the trunk and outline of the tree.

**2** Draw the main branches. Make each branch thick near the trunk and thinner at the ends.

**3** Use different shades of green for the leaves. Make the top leaves pale and the lower leaves dark, where it is more shady.

**Click for Art!**

To see a landscape by Monet, go to **www.ibiblio.org/wm/paint/auth/monet/** and click on "First Impressionist paintings."

# Still life

A still life is a drawing or painting of something that does not move, such as flowers in a vase or a bowl of fruit.

**1** Take time arranging the fruit in a bowl or on a tabletop until you are happy with the way it looks.

**2** Lightly sketch the outline of the bowl first, then draw the fruit. Start with the pieces at the front of the bowl.

### You will need:

- Something to draw, such as a bowl of fruit or a flower
- Colored pencils, chalks, crayons, or pastels

**Tiny lines give the orange peel a rough texture**

**Shading makes the fruit look rounded and three-dimensional**

**3** Draw the pieces of fruit at the back. Only draw the parts of the fruit you can see.

**4** Go over your outlines in crayon, chalk, or pastel.

**5** Color in or shade your picture (see page 6 for ideas).

## Top tip

Before you start, look carefully at what you are going to draw. It sounds obvious, but many people who try to draw don't do that!

**A colorful still life of flowers in a vase.**

**Click for Art!**

To see still life paintings by Cézanne, go to **www.ibiblio.org/wm/paint/auth/cezanne/sl/**

23

# Glossary

**background**   area behind the subject of a picture, such as distant hills behind the figure of a horse

**features**   parts of the face, such as the eyes, nose, and mouth, that make each person look different

**highlights**   bright parts of a picture where there is no shading

**outline**   the outer shape of an object; usually you draw the outline first, then add in the details

**pastel paper**   thick, textured paper available in different colors

**shading**   adding darker areas to a drawing to make it more realistic

**sketch paper**   thick, smooth paper for pencil drawings and paintings

**sketchbook**   a small, easy-to-carry book for making quick drawings and designs

**texture**   the surface or "feel" of something: for example, rough, soft, furry, bumpy, smooth, or velvety

**three-dimensional (3-D)**   when something has height, width, and depth, instead of just being flat

# Index